MASTERING SAFETY HARNESS

From **compliance** to **comfort** , a **comprehensive** guide

MASTERING SAFETY HARNESS

From **compliance** to **comfort**, a **comprehensive** guide

Ashish K Mittal

Worldwide Published by

Pendown Press

PENDOWN PRESS LLP
An ISO 9001 & ISO 14001 Certified Co.,
Regd. Office: 3767A, Kanhaiya Nagar,
Tri Nagar, Delhi-110035
Ph.: 8130886000, 9650072927
E-mail: info@pendownpress.com
Branch Office: 1A/2A, 20, Hari Sadan, Ansari Road,
Daryaganj, New Delhi-110002
Ph.: 011-45794768
Website: PendownPress.com

Edition: 2025

ISBN: 978-93-6338-033-2

Layout and Cover Designed by Pendown Graphics Team
Printed and Bound in India by Thomson Press India Ltd.

To every worker who dedicates their time and energy to making the world a safer, stronger place. Your efforts often go unseen, but they are truly invaluable. Your commitment to safety and well-being inspires this journey toward better, smarter protection.

Thank you for all that you do.

Table of Contents

Acknowledgements

My parents, Mr. Krishan Mittal and Mrs. Anita Mittal, are my greatest role models. Their unwavering love, guidance, and values have brought me to where I am today. I am truly grateful for everything they have done.

To my wife, Reema Mittal, who has stood by me in every situation. You have handled all family responsibilities with great skill and dedication. Thank you from the bottom of my heart.

To my children, Atharv and Shridhi Mittal, who are the source of my happiness and inspiration. Sending you lots of love!

To my team at I SSAFE, who have been like partners, mentors, and family. Thank you for walking this journey with me.

To our customers, who have shared their experiences and knowledge with us during this journey—thank you for trusting us and being our inspiration.

To my friend, Mr. Dinesh Verma, CEO of Pendown Press, and his team, who supported us throughout this creative process and provided great suggestions.

To the universe for giving me the ideas and strength to complete this book. I am grateful for the love, support, and guidance at every step.

And finally, to all my loved ones who have been with me on this journey—thank you for your unwavering support, encouragement, and affection. Even if your names are not mentioned, you always hold a special place in my heart.

Without the support of all of you, it would not have been possible for me to move forward with confidence.

❍❍❍❍

Preface

Welcome! First off, thank you for picking up this book. Whether you're new to safety harnesses or looking to refine your knowledge, you're in the right place. This book is designed to be simple, straightforward, and easy to understand—no complex jargon or overwhelming technicalities.

If you're reading this, you're probably working in an industry where safety is a top priority. We all know that harnesses are more than just safety gear—they're a lifeline. Over the years, safety harnesses have evolved, becoming more comfortable, durable, and adaptable. But there's a lot more to it than just strapping on a harness. The right harness can make a world of difference in terms of comfort, safety, and even productivity.

In the following pages, I'll Walk you through everything you need to know, from the basic components of a harness to the latest innovations in the field. Whether you're a manufacturer, an employer, or a worker, I want to help you make informed decisions about the equipment you rely on.

By the end of this book, you'll be equipped not only with the knowledge to choose the best safety harnesses but also the insights to foster a safer, more comfortable work environment.

So, let's dive in, and together, let's make safety a priority!

Best Wishes,

Ashish K Mittal

Overview

Safety is crucial when working at heights, yet it's often misunderstood. *"Mastering Safety Harnesses: From Compliance to Comfort, A Comprehensive Guide"* sheds light on the vital role safety harnesses—not just as a regulatory requirement but as a critical life-saving tool.

This takes you on a unique journey from the history and development of safety harnesses to the latest innovations and standards in design and functionality. Authored by an industry expert who transitioned from a career in textile weaving to becoming a pioneer in safety harness technology, this guide provides unmatched insights into the materials, designs, and engineering that go into making safety harnesses reliable and effective.

Readers will explore important but often-overlooked aspects of safety harness usage, like why ergonomic design matters, how stitching and belt width affect performance, and how to balance strength with ease of use. The book shares five key tips for selecting the right harness, along with practical advice and by real-world examples backed by technological expertise.

Moreover, "Mastering Safety Harnesses" addresses common problems faced by users, such as discomfort during long hours of wear or difficulty finding the right fit, and offers smart solutions along with tips for proper maintenance and care. With safety rules constantly changing, this book is also a helpful resource for understanding compliance and the legal responsibilities of using safety equipment.

Whether you're a site manager, a safety equipment designer, a construction worker, or simply involved in any industry requiring safety at heights, this comprehensive guide is your go-to resource for improving safety standards and practices. By the time you finish this book, you will not only have a thorough understanding of how to choose and use safety harnesses but also appreciate the significant role these devices play in saving lives.

"Mastering Safety Harnesses" is more than just a book; it's an essential tool in the mission to elevate safety and ensure that every climb upwards is secure and every worker returns safely.

From Threads to Safety: My Journey to Harness Expertise

My journey in the world of safety began not in the clouds among the high-rise structures of modern industry, but at the very fabric of construction — literally. Born into a family of weavers, I grew up surrounded by the sounds of narrow woven looms and the art of textile patterns. As a second-generation entrepreneur, the fabric of innovation and industry was woven into my very being. My father, a pioneer in textile manufacturing, taught me the value of craftsmanship, quality, and attention to detail.

Over the past 34 years, my career has taken a significant shift from textiles to safety, with a focus exclusively on manufacturing safety harnesses. This change was sparked by my realization of the growing need for specialized safety equipment, especially in the high-risk environments of modern construction and industrial work, where safety at heights is a major concern. Today, I now lead India's only company dedicated solely to producing safety harnesses. This unique position speaks to our deep commitment and expertise in ensuring safety and protection in industries where height and risk go hand in hand.

Our commitment to excellence is evidenced by our certifications. We are proud to be BIS (INDIAN CERTIFICATION), CE (EUROPEAN CERTIFICATION) and ANSI (AMERICAN CERTIFICATION) certified. This international recognition is a testament to our stringent quality standards and our adherence to global best practices in safety. Additionally, our products are accredited and approved by NBCC, marking us as a trusted partner to one of the largest oil and gas enterprises in Asia.

At the core of our operations is a dedicated team of over 550 professionals, including my son, Ashish K Mittal, who has been with the company for 19 years. Together, we bring a wealth of knowledge and expertise in safety harness manufacturing, continuously innovating and improving our products to meet the diverse needs of our clients.

Our manufacturing line, which can be viewed in detailed video presentations, giving customers an inside look at how each harness is made. These videos not only demonstrate our commitment to transparency but also educate our customers about the rigorous steps we take to ensure every harness meets the highest standards of safety and comfort. Our vision is clear: we aim to expand the reach of the company, advance harness technology, and raise industry standards, ultimately ensuring that every worker who straps into a harness can trust its safety and reliability.

Our philosophy is simple yet profound: **"हम सिर्फ हार्नेस नहीं; हम सेफ्टी हार्नेस ही बनाते हैं"** (We don't just make harnesses; we make only safety harnesses). This statement reflects our dedication to quality, innovation, and protecting workers. It's more than just a motto—it represents our mission to provide workers with equipment they can rely on, a commitment that has helped us lead the way in this field.

Looking ahead, my vision is clear. We want to grow our reach, improve our technology, and continue to educate and provide industries with the best safety solutions. Our goal is to make sure every worker can confidently climb and come back safely each day.

The introduction wraps up by setting an optimistic and collaborative tone, inviting readers on a journey through the intricate world of safety harnesses—from historical evolution and technical components to future advancements and cultural shifts in safety.

The author's passion and expertise establish a strong foundation, encouraging readers to engage with each chapter, equipped with practical advice, insights, and a shared dedication to the highest safety standards.

Chapter 1

The Critical Role of Safety Harnesses

1.1 Introduction to Safety Harnesses as Life-Saving Tools

The True Purpose of Safety Harnesses

Safety harnesses are not simply items of workwear; they are meticulously engineered tools designed to save lives and reduce the risks associated with working at heights. For workers across various sectors—from construction and industrial maintenance to telecommunications and oil rigs—harnesses serve as a crucial line of defence, ensuring their safety and enabling them to perform demanding tasks in high-risk environments. Despite the clear benefits, many people see them merely as a box to check for regulatory compliance, overlooking their importance as essential life-saving equipment.

1.2 Types of Safety Harnesses

1. Body Belts

- **Description:** A simple belt worn around the waist.
- **Specialization Field:** Work positioning and restraint systems.

- **Usage:** Used for restriction or positioning to prevent a worker from leaning too far or falling. Commonly employed in maintenance, scaffolding, and platform work.
- **Limitations:** Not suitable for fall arrest systems due to the risk of injury from concentrated pressure during a fall.

2. **Full-Body Harnesses**

- **Description:** Encompasses the shoulders, thighs, and torso, distributing fall forces across the body.
- **Specialization Field:** General fall protection across various industries.
- **Usage:** Ideal for fall arrest, work positioning, suspension, and climbing. Commonly used in construction, roofing, and telecommunications.
- **Key Features:**
    - **D-Rings:** Attachment points for lanyards and lifelines, (typically located on the dorsal side, front, sides, or lower back).
    - **Padding:** Enhances comfort during extended long-term use.
    - **Certifications:** Compliant with standards such as ANSI, CE, and ISI.

3. **Suspension Harnesses**

- **Description:** Designed for work requiring suspension in the air.
- **Specialization Field:** Rope access, rescue operations, and industrial cleaning.

- **Usage:** Suitable for tasks like window cleaning, tower painting, and rescue missions where suspension is necessary.
- **Key Features:**
  - Added support for thighs and lower body.
  - Front D-rings for connection to suspension systems.

4. **Positioning Harnesses**
   - **Description:** Keeps workers in place while leaving hands free for tasks.
   - **Specialization Field:** Construction and utility work.
   - **Usage:** Utility pole work, scaffolding, and bridge construction. Suitable for tasks that require stability while working at heights.
   - **Key Features:**
     - Side D-rings for restraint and positioning.
     - Not suitable for free-fall arrest.

5. **Retrieval/Rescue Harnesses**
   - **Description:** Designed for confined space entry or rescue operations.
   - **Specialization Field:** Emergency response and confined space operations.
   - **Usage:** Rescue from tanks, manholes, or similar environments. Commonly used by firefighters and industrial safety teams.
   - **Key Features:**
     - Additional attachment points for vertical extraction.
     - Lightweight for ease of movement.

6. **Climbing Harnesses**

   - **Description:** Specialized harnesses for ladder climbing or vertical ascents.

   - **Specialization Field:** Tower climbing and wind energy.

   - **Usage:** Telecom towers, wind turbines, and high-rise construction. Designed for safe and secure climbing activities.

   - **Key Features:**

     - Front or sternal D-ring for ladder fall arresters.

     - Secure fit to prevent shifting during climbs.

7. **Fall Arrest Harnesses**

   - **Description**: Aimed at stopping a fall and minimizing impact forces on the body.

   - **Specialization Field**: General height safety across industries.

   - **Usage**: Construction, roofing, scaffolding, and heavy machinery work. Designed to arrest falls effectively while minimizing bodily harm.

   - **Key Features:**

     - Dorsal D-ring for shock-absorbing lanyard or retractable lifeline attachment.

     - Energy absorbers for reduced impact.

8. **Specialized Harnesses**

   - **Fire-Resistant Harnesses**:

     - **Specialization Field**: Hot work environments like welding and foundries.

- **Usage**: Protects workers in environments with high heat or fire hazards.
- **Arc-Flash Rated Harnesses**:
  - **Specialization Field**: Electrical and powerline work.
  - **Usage**: Protects against electrical arc flashes in high-voltage operations.
- **Women's Safety Harnesses**:
  - **Specialization Field**: Gender-specific ergonomics for female workers.
  - **Usage**: Ensures comfort and safety for women working at heights.

9. **Multi-Purpose Harnesses**
   - **Description**: Combines features of various types for versatile use.
   - **Specialization Field**: Flexible use across multi-functional work environments.
   - **Usage**: Ideal for industries requiring a mix of fall arrest, positioning, and suspension, such as oil and gas or utility maintenance.
   - **Key Features**:
     - Adjustable straps for diverse body sizes.
     - Multiple D-ring options for various tasks.

10. **Specialty Harness Designs**
    - **Cross-Chest Harnesses**:
      - **Specialization Field**: Long-duration tasks requiring high comfort.

- **Usage**: Suitable for industrial climbing and long-term suspension work.

- **Tower Harnesses**:

  - **Specialization Field**: Telecom and power transmission towers.

  - **Usage**: Equipped for both fall arrest and climbing activities.

- **Industrial Harnesses**:

  - **Specialization Field**: Heavy-duty applications in construction and mining.

  - **Usage**: Built for rugged environments with reinforced stitching and robust materials.

1.3 Differentiating Life-Saving Uses from Mere Compliance

Compliance Versus Commitment to Safety

Many organizations view safety harnesses primarily as a means of meeting regulatory requirements, adhering to OSHA (Occupational Safety and Health Administration) and ANSI (American National Standards Institute) standards. While compliance is important, the true power of safety harnesses lies in their ability to prevent injuries and save lives. When used properly and designed with care, harnesses can significantly reduce injury rates. Businesses need to move beyond viewing them as just a rule to follow and instead embrace their role in worker safety.

Statistics That Speak the Truth

➢ **OSHA Statistics:** According to OSHA, falls are the leading cause of death in construction, with 351 fatal falls recorded in the construction industry in 2020 alone (OSHA, 2021). A large percentage of these incidents could have been prevented with proper harness use and equipment maintenance. Insert Source: OSHA 2021 Report on Fall Protection

➢ **ANSI Data:** ANSI reports show that fall-related injuries cost industries billions of dollars annually due to lost productivity, compensation, and liability. This substantial financial toll highlights the necessity of a strong safety harness program, not just for worker safety but for long-term cost savings for businesses. Insert Source: ANSI Fall Protection Standards

➢ **Economic Costs of Falls:** According to a 28 November 2023 report, $50 billion is spent annually on medical costs for older adult falls, with Medicare alone covering $29 billion for non-fatal falls. These figures highlight the far-reaching financial burden of falls, both in and out of the workplace.

Time Lost Due to Work-Related Injuries (2022 Data)

The 108,000,000 days lost in 2022 are a result of injuries that occurred in 2022 and days lost in 2022 from injuries that occurred in previous years.

Days lost due to injuries in 2022 totaled 75,000,000. This estimate includes the actual time lost during the year from disabling injuries, but excludes time lost on the day of the injury, time required for further medical treatment, or check-ups following the injured person's return to work.

Fatalities are calculated with an average loss of 150 days per case, and permanent impairments are included as actual days lost, plus an allowance for reduced efficiency resulting from the impairment.

An additional 33,000,000 days were lost in 2022 due to permanently disabling injuries that occurred in prior years.

The National Safety Council (NSC) estimates that 60,000,000 additional days will be lost in future years due to on-the-job deaths and permanently disabling injuries that occurred in 2022.

1.4   The Reality of Working at Heights

Worker Perspective

For workers operating on tall structures, safety harnesses are not just about compliance—they are about trust and reliability. Many workers share how vital it is to feel safe while wearing a harness, knowing that it's designed to hold their weight, cushion the impact of a fall, and evenly spread the force across their body to minimize injury.

1.5   Real-World Case Studies: Harnesses as Life-Saving Equipment

Case Study 1: Construction Industry

A notable case study involves a major U.S. construction company that implemented a strict harness policy, mandating certified equipment for every worker operating at heights. Within a year, their incident reports dropped by 47%, and injuries were reduced significantly. This case illustrates the practical impact of investing in high-quality harnesses and the effect of prioritizing safety beyond regulatory mandates.

Case Study 2: Telecommunications Industry

Workers in the telecommunications sector frequently face the dangers of working on high cellular towers and structures. A 2019 study by the Telecommunications Safety Association reported a 30% reduction in fatalities when companies provided updated, ergonomically designed harnesses with back support and anti-shock features. This case underscores the importance of modernizing safety equipment to address specific risks and improve worker protection.

1.6 Moving Beyond Compliance: Building a Safety-First Mindset

Creating a Culture of Safety

Focusing on safety isn't just about meeting legal requirements—it's about genuinely caring for workers' well-being. Steps like providing safety training, conducting regular equipment checks, and investing in well-designed, ergonomic harnesses show employees that their safety is a top priority. While these initiatives may seem like an added cost, they are minor compared to the financial savings and trust earned by reducing workplace accidents.

Practical Steps for Organizations

➢ **Invest in Quality:** High-quality harnesses that meet or exceed ANSI standards are essential. Companies should look for harnesses that provide comfort and are tested for durability under different conditions.

➢ **Ongoing Training:** Regular training on proper harness usage can reduce misuse and accidents.

➢ **Scheduled Inspections:** Routine inspections help identify worn or damaged -harnesses, preventing accidents.

1.7　The Takeaway: Why Safety Harnesses Are Non-Negotiable

The message is simple: safety harnesses are not just another line item on a safety checklist—they are indispensable tools that save lives. This chapter's data, case studies, and real-world perspectives underscore the essential role of harnesses in workplace safety. Prioritizing safety isn't about ticking a box; it's about safeguarding the well-being of employees, who are the backbone of every organization. Making safety a priority is not an option—it's a responsibility every employer must embrace to ensure their people stay safe and return home every day.

Chapter 2

Historical Development of Safety Harnesses

2.1 Introduction: The Evolution of Safety Harness Design

Safety harnesses have come a long way, evolving from simple straps and belts to today's sophisticated, ergonomically designed equipment. The history of these harnesses reflects not only advances in materials and engineering but also a deepening understanding of worker safety and the importance of comfort in high-risk jobs. This chapter takes you through the key milestones in harness development, offering readers a comprehensive look at how harnesses have transformed from basic fall-arrest tools to the modern, life-saving devices used in diverse industries today.

2.2 Early Safety Measures: From Ropes to Belts

The Beginnings of Fall Protection (1900s–1950s)

In the early 20th century, safety measures for workers at heights were very basic. Construction workers, painters, and linemen often relied on ropes tied around their waists or rudimentary leather belts to prevent falls. These solutions were rudimentary at best, designed to catch a worker after a fall rather than provide any form of shock absorption or ergonomic support.

In the 1940s, basic belts made from leather or woven canvas were adopted by high-rise construction workers and linemen, particularly in industries like bridge building and telecommunications. While these belts could stop a worker from hitting the ground, they didn't absorb shock or protect the body from the impact forces of a fall. Injuries to the spine or internal organs were common, as the focus back then was simply to prevent the fall, not to reduce the damage caused by it.

A historical photograph of bridge construction workers using early fall protection belts in the 1930s.

Golden Gate Bridge Construction Safety Practices

The construction of San Francisco's Golden Gate Bridge began in the 1930's. At the time of construction, expectations were that one person would die for every $1 million spent. Joseph Strauss, chief project engineer, implemented revolutionary safety practices for that time. Strauss required workers to wear hard hats and safety belts with tie off lines and to use respirators during riveting.

Three years into construction, Strauss invested more than $130,000 for a rope-and-mesh safety net suspended under the bridge. This net gave those working on the bridge confidence to move across the construction of the bridge's roadway and prevented deadly falls. During construction, 19 workers fell into the net and survived, earning them the nickname "Halfway to Hell Club." Tragically, on February 16, 1937, a five-ton platform collapsed, ripping through the net. As a result, 12 men fell 220 feet into the water. Ten of the 12 workers died from the fall. Only 11 workers died during the entire project, but without the net and other safety requirements, that number could have been much higher.

Strauss' original plan included safety railing installation to prevent suicides from the Golden Gate Bridge. According to Strauss' guardrail plan: "five feet, six inches high and are so constructed that any persons on the pedestrian walk could not get a handhold to climb over them." However, architect Irving Morrow revised this design, lowering the rails to four feet and spacing the posts further apart. While this alteration aligned with aesthetic goals, it reduced the guardrails' effectiveness in preventing suicides after the bridge's opening in May 1937.

2.3   The Rise of Full-Body Harnesses

Introduction of the Full-Body Harness (960s–1970s)

The 1960s marked a turning point in safety harness design. There was growing awareness that harnesses needed to distribute the force of a fall more evenly across the body to reduce the risk of injury. Early prototypes of full-body harnesses, originally developed for the military, made their way into civilian industries, particularly construction and forestry. These designs were inspired by parachute harnesses, which distributed force across the torso, hips, and legs, reducing the risk of injury from concentrated impact.

In the 1970s, ANSI began establishing standards for fall protection equipment, including full-body harnesses. This era saw the development of harnesses with basic padding and reinforced stitching, aimed at both safety and a minimal level of user comfort. These harnesses still lacked the ergonomic features present in today's models, but they represented a significant improvement in fall protection.

2.4   Technological Milestones and Industry Standards

Advancements in Materials and Design (1980s–1990s)

The 1980s brought substantial innovations in the materials used for harnesses. Nylon and polyester fibers replaced the earlier materials, providing greater strength, durability, and resistance to weather conditions. The use of these synthetic fibers allowed manufacturers to design lighter, stronger, and more flexible harnesses that improved worker mobility and comfort. Moreover, these materials provided resistance against wear and tear from outdoor elements, extending harness lifespan and reliability.

During this period, both ANSI and OSHA developed more comprehensive standards for safety harnesses, focusing on criteria such as tensile strength, durability, and shock absorption capacity. These standards focused on important qualities like tensile strength (how much force a harness could handle), durability, and shock absorption, ensuring that harnesses could withstand the challenges of different work environments. This led to stricter quality checks, guaranteeing better safety for workers.

Integration of Ergonomics (1990s–2000s)

In the 1990s, ergonomics became a critical consideration in harness design, as workers began to complain about discomfort, limited movement, and fatigue from wearing them for long periods. To address these issues, new harness designs included padding in key areas, such as the shoulders, thighs, and back, to distribute pressure more evenly and reduce discomfort during extended use. Adjustable buckles and snap hooks allowed for customized fit, accommodating a wider range of body types and work situations.

This era also saw the advent of harnesses designed for specific industries, such as telecommunications, oil and gas, and utilities, where the needs for flexibility, durability, and safety varied. Manufacturers began incorporating additional safety features like shock-absorbing lanyards and energy-dissipating systems to minimize injury risks further.

2.5 Modern Innovations and Smart Technology

The Rise of Smart Harnesses and Real-Time Monitoring (2010s–Present)

Today, technological advances have introduced "smart harnesses," equipped with sensors that can monitor the worker's position, detect falls, and trigger alerts in real time. Some of these harnesses even come with GPS technology, enabling site managers to monitor workers' locations and movement patterns remotely, which is especially valuable in large industrial sites and high-rise projects. These innovations are transforming the role of harnesses from simple safety equipment into active, real-time safety systems that work to prevent accidents before they happen.

Research and development in material science continue to enhance the durability and functionality of harnesses. New, high-strength, lightweight polymers and weather-resistant coatings are making harnesses more resilient and adaptable to harsh working environments. Companies are also experimenting with harnesses made from eco-friendly, sustainable materials, reflecting a broader industry shift toward environmental responsibility.

2.6 Future of Safety Harness Design

The future of safety harnesses is likely to be shaped by continued advancements in both ergonomic design and digital technology integration. Industry leaders predict that wearable technologies—such as harnesses capable of monitoring vital signs, hydration levels, and muscle fatigue—will become standard in high-risk environments. These features could help prevent accidents by alerting workers when they are physically overextended or fatigued, addressing one of the root causes of falls.

In addition, 3D printing technology may allow for customized harness production, tailored to the specific body measurements of each worker, ensuring an optimal fit and enhanced comfort. This level of customization could mark the next significant evolution in safety harness manufacturing, supporting the industry's shift toward prioritizing worker well-being and satisfaction.

2.7 Conclusion: The Journey from Simple Belts to Smart Harnesses

The evolution of safety harnesses is a testament to the safety industry's ongoing commitment to protecting workers and improving their work experience. From the early days of basic belts to today's advanced smart harnesses, each stage of development has brought us closer to a future where safety harnesses do more than just prevent falls—they actively contribute to a safer, healthier, and more sustainable work environment.

This journey underscores a powerful truth: as technology advances, so does our ability to protect and empower workers at every level, ensuring they are equipped not just for compliance but for life-saving comfort and reliability.

○　○　○　○

Chapter 3

Misuses and Misconceptions

3.1 Introduction: Addressing Common Misuses and Misunderstandings

Safety harnesses are one of the most important tools to prevent falls at work, but they only work well if used correctly. Unfortunately, misconceptions about harnesses are common, leading to improper use and, ultimately, compromised safety. Misunderstandings about harness features, capabilities, and limitations can have severe consequences, especially when workers put their lives at risk believing they are fully protected. This chapter addresses the most prevalent misconceptions about safety harnesses, highlights dangerous misuses, and provides guidance on how to avoid these pitfalls.

3.2 Misconception #1: "Any Harness is Better Than No Harness"

The Danger of Overconfidence in Non-Approved Equipment

One of the most widespread misconceptions is that any harness, regardless of type or certification, provides adequate protection. Not all harnesses are made the same, and using one that isn't approved or properly maintained can lead to serious risks. Harnesses that are outdated or not up to safety standards may not be strong enough to stop a fall in time. In fact, a report from OSHA in 2021 revealed that about 20% of fall-related deaths happened while workers were using harnesses that were either uncertified or in poor condition, causing them to fail when needed the most.

3.3 Misconception #2: "One Size Fits All"

The Critical Importance of Proper Fit

Another dangerous misconception is that safety harnesses are "one size fits all." In reality, a harness must be correctly sized and adjusted to provide proper protection. A poorly fitted harness can lead to discomfort, reduced mobility, and even serious injury if it fails to secure the worker during a fall. Research from the National Institute for Occupational Safety and Health (NIOSH) reveals that ill-fitting harnesses contribute to 15% of fall-related injuries, often due to straps slipping or failing to engage properly (NIOSH, 2020).

(www.issafe.in)

3.4 Misconception #3: "All Harnesses Provide Fall Protection"

Differentiating Between Positioning, Restraint, and Fall-Arrest Harnesses

Many users assume that any harness will protect them from falls. However, there are distinct types of harnesses designed for different applications: positioning, restraint, and fall arrest. Each type serves a specific purpose, and misuse can lead to catastrophic outcomes. Positioning harnesses, for example, are intended to keep a worker stable but may not withstand the forces of a fall. According to a 2019 report by the American Society of Safety Professionals (ASSP), over 25% of fall-related incidents occurred when workers mistakenly used positioning harnesses instead of fall-arrest harnesses in high-risk environments (ASSP, 2019).

3.5 Misconception #4: "Harnesses Don't Require Regular Maintenance"

The Importance of Regular Inspections and Maintenance

A common oversight is believing that safety harnesses are "maintenance-free." Regular inspections are crucial to identify signs of wear and tear, such as frayed straps, rusted buckles, and weakened stitching, which can compromise the harness's integrity. According to OSHA guidelines, safety harnesses should be inspected before each use and undergo thorough examination at least once a year by a qualified inspector (OSHA, 2021).

3.6 Misconception #5: "Harnesses Are Only Necessary for High-Rise Work"

Risks Exist Even at Lower Heights

Some workers and employers mistakenly believe that harnesses are only needed when working at extreme heights. However, studies have shown that fatal falls can occur from heights as low as 6 feet. OSHA mandates that fall protection is required for heights of 4 feet in general industry workplaces and 6 feet in the construction industry (OSHA, 2021).

3.7 Conclusion: Correcting Misconceptions, Saving Lives

Misuses and misconceptions about safety harnesses are not just issues of ignorance; they are potentially life-threatening misunderstandings that can lead to fatal errors. By understanding the distinct types of harnesses, prioritizing proper fit and regular maintenance, and recognizing the need for protection even at lower heights, workers and employers can prevent unnecessary risks. A commitment to training, education, and ongoing equipment inspection forms the foundation of a safe workplace where every worker can trust their harness to perform as intended.

Chapter 4

The Mechanics of Safety Harnesses

4.1 Introduction: Understanding the Structure and Purpose of Safety Harnesses

Safety harnesses are meticulously designed devices, engineered to distribute the force of a fall and prevent injury. While they may appear simple, harnesses consist of multiple components, each with a critical role in protecting workers at heights. To understand the true value of a safety harness, it's essential to examine the mechanics and function of each part, from the webbing and buckles to the D-rings and padding. This chapter dives into the components and design principles that make modern harnesses effective tools for fall prevention, helping readers appreciate the technology behind these life-saving devices.

4.2 Components of a Safety Harness

Each component of a safety harness plays a specific role in ensuring security, comfort, and functionality. Here, we break down the essential parts and explore how they contribute to the overall effectiveness of a harness.

4.3 Webbing: The Backbone of Safety Harnesses

Material Science and Strength

The webbing in a safety harness is the most important part that carries the weight and helps protect workers during a fall. Modern harnesses often use high-strength materials like nylon or polyester, known for their durability, flexibility, and resistance to weather conditions. According to ANSI standards, the webbing in a harness should be able to handle at least 5,000 pounds of force to make sure it works properly during a fall (ANSI Z359.1, 2021).

Nylon webbing, commonly used in industrial harnesses, is valued for its stretch and shock absorption capabilities. Polyester, on the other hand, offers higher UV and water resistance, making it suitable for outdoor and high-moisture environments. These materials are also tested for chemical resistance to ensure they remain safe in various work environments.

4.4   D-Rings: The Critical Connectors

Understanding D-Ring Placement and Function

D-rings are the primary attachment points in a harness, linking the user to lanyards, lifelines, or anchor points. The most common is the dorsal D-ring, which sits between the shoulder blades. This D-ring helps keep the worker upright during a fall, making sure they don't flip upside down. According to ANSI, D-rings must be strong enough to handle at least 5,000 pounds of force to prevent them from breaking in an accident (ANSI Z359.1, 2021).

Additional D-rings may be located on the hips, chest, or waist, depending on the harness model and intended use. Hip D-rings, for example, allow for positioning and stability, giving workers greater control when operating in confined spaces or on inclined surfaces. Chest D-rings are often included in harnesses designed for ladder climbing, allowing workers to stay secure while using both hands.

4.5 Buckles: Ensuring Secure Fit and Adjustment

Types of Buckles and Their Role

Buckles are a key part of a safety harness, helping to securely attach the harness to the worker's body. They are designed for easy adjustment to achieve a snug fit, reducing the risk of slipping or shifting. The three main types of buckles used in safety harnesses are:

➢ **Tongue Buckles:** Resembling belt buckles, tongue buckles provide a secure fit and are commonly used around the waist or leg straps.

➢ **Quick-Connect Buckles:** Like seatbelt buckles, these are fast to use, making them ideal for situations where workers need to put the harness on and take it off frequently.

➢ **Parachute Buckles:** These offer incremental adjustments, allowing a customized fit to accommodate different body sizes and clothing layers.

Incorrectly adjusted buckles can lead to discomfort and even injury. For example, loose straps may allow a worker to slip out of the harness, while overly tight straps can restrict movement and cause circulation issues. ANSI standards specify that all buckles must be tested for impact resistance and durability (ANSI Z359.11, 2021).

4.6 Padding: Enhancing Comfort for Extended Use

The Role of Padding in Ergonomic Design

Padding has become an essential component in harnesses, especially for workers who wear them for extended periods. Positioned around the shoulders, waist, and legs, padding helps distribute pressure evenly, reducing strain and improving comfort. Ergonomic research shows that padded harnesses can reduce muscle fatigue by up to 30%, making them valuable for jobs that require prolonged use, such as tower maintenance or construction (NIOSH, 2020).

Modern harnesses use breathable, moisture-wicking materials in their padding to prevent heat buildup, which can lead to skin irritation and discomfort. By enhancing comfort, padding not only makes harnesses more wearable but also encourages compliance, as workers are less likely to neglect wearing uncomfortable equipment.

4.7 Stitching and Load-Bearing Integrity

Why Stitching Matters

Stitching quality is a critical but often overlooked aspect of safety harness design. Harness stitching needs to be strong enough to handle the huge forces during a fall. ANSI standards require that stitching be tested to withstand a minimum tensile load of 5,000 pounds, the same as the webbing and D-rings (ANSI Z359.1, 2021).

Harnesses with contrasting stitching, where different-colored threads make inspection easier, are preferred in many industries because they make it easier to check for damage.

This feature allows users to detect fraying or damaged stitches more readily, ensuring they can replace the harness before it becomes unsafe. Double and triple-stitching patterns are common in high-quality harnesses, as they add additional strength to high-stress areas.

4.8   The Role of Design Principles in Safety and Functionality

Balancing Safety and User Experience

Modern harness design focus on both safety and ergonomics. An effective harness not only prevents falls but also minimizes the risk of injury by distributing forces across the body and accommodating natural movement. Factors such as adjustable straps, proper D-ring placement, and breathable padding all contribute to a harness's functionality and wearability.

Many manufacturers now use computer modeling to simulate the forces exerted on different body parts during a fall. These simulations help engineers refine harness designs to minimize the physical strain on the wearer. A 2021 study by the American Society of Mechanical Engineers (ASME) found that ergonomic harnesses can reduce "suspension trauma"—the discomfort caused by hanging for too long—by up to 40%, making them safer for workers who need to stay suspended for extended periods.

4.9 Conclusion: The Anatomy of Protection

Safety harnesses are more than mere collections of straps and buckles; they are complex devices designed to protect lives. By understanding the mechanics behind each component and how these parts work together, workers and safety professionals can make informed choices about harness selection, use, and maintenance. This knowledge empowers users to appreciate the importance of every element in a harness, from the webbing material to the stitching quality, ensuring they select equipment that not only meets safety standards but also provides comfort and reliability.

Chapter 5

Weaving Science into Safety

5.1 Introduction: The Intersection of Textile Engineering and Safety

Every safety harness is built around specially designed textile material, carefully woven to provide strength, flexibility, and resilience. The evolution of harness webbing shows how textile engineering and material science have advanced, allowing manufacturers to create harnesses that can handle extreme forces while keeping the user comfortable and mobile. This chapter examines the weaving techniques, material properties, and engineering principles that make safety harnesses effective, reliable, and comfortable for users in high-risk environments.

5.2 The Importance of Webbing in Safety Harnesses

Why Webbing Matters

Webbing is the core of any safety harness, designed to bear the brunt of force exerted during a fall. Harness webbing is typically crafted from synthetic fibers such as nylon and polyester, chosen for their durability, tensile strength, and resistance to environmental factors like UV rays, moisture, and abrasion. The strength and integrity of webbing are vital for harness performance, as weak or damaged webbing can lead to harness failure.

According to ANSI standards, harness webbing must withstand at least 5,000 pounds of tensile load, reflecting the importance of robust weaving techniques (ANSI Z359.1, 2021).

5.3 Materials Science: The Building Blocks of Strong Webbing

Nylon and Polyester: Characteristics and Applications

Nylon and polyester are the two primary materials used in harness webbing due to their high strength-to-weight ratios and environmental resistance. Nylon offers elasticity, which helps absorb shock during a fall, while polyester provides greater UV and moisture resistance, making it ideal for outdoor applications.

➢ **Nylon Webbing:** Known for its flexibility and stretch, nylon can absorb energy, providing a cushion effect in the event of a fall. This material is frequently used in harnesses where some degree of elasticity is beneficial.

➢ **Polyester Webbing:** Polyester is less elastic than nylon but offers enhanced durability in outdoor conditions. It resists UV degradation and retains its strength when wet, which makes it ideal for environments exposed to sunlight or moisture.

5.4 The Weaving Techniques Behind Stronger, Safer Harnesses

Understanding the Weave Pattern

The structure of the weave—whether plain, twill, or satin—

impacts the strength, flexibility, and durability of the harness webbing. Different weaving techniques distribute force and wear differently, which is crucial for applications involving regular movement and stress.

➢ **Plain Weave:** This is the simplest weave where the fibers cross over and under in a regular pattern. This pattern creates a stable and strong fabric with minimal stretch, commonly used in safety harnesses where rigidity is required.

➢ **Twill Weave:** In twill weaving, the fibers are arranged in a diagonal pattern, which adds flexibility while maintaining strength. Twill weaves are often used in harnesses that require both strength and some flexibility.

➢ **Satin Weave:** While less common in safety applications, satin weaves provide a smoother surface that reduces friction wear, which can be beneficial for certain high-movement applications.

Diagram of different weave patterns (plain, twill, satin), showing structural differences.

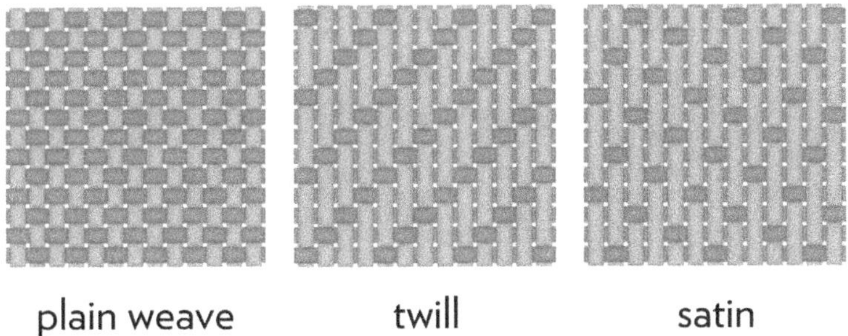

Industry Insight

A report published by the Textile Institute in 2019 found

that twill-weave harnesses exhibited 15% more flexibility than plain-weave harnesses, with no significant loss in tensile strength. The report recommended twill weaves for harnesses used in applications where worker mobility is a priority, such as telecommunications.

5.5 Reinforcement Techniques: Adding Strength Through Layering and Stitching

Layered Weaving and Stitching for Extra Durability

Harnesses often use layered webbing and reinforced stitching to increase strength and load-bearing capacity. In high-stress areas, such as connection points, additional layers of webbing are applied, and stitching patterns are reinforced to distribute force evenly.

Double and triple-stitching patterns are common in harnesses, providing extra security in areas subject to high stress. In particular, bar-tack stitching, a method where short, close-set stitches form a compact line, is widely used in safety harnesses to secure webbing layers. This method has been shown to increase a harness's load-bearing capacity by up to 25%, according to a 2021 study by the American Society of Mechanical Engineers (ASME).

Close-up image of bar-tack stitching on harness webbing, highlighting the density and precision of the stitching.

5.6 Conclusion: The Science of Weaving for Safety

The materials and weaving techniques used in harness webbing are critical factors in determining a harness's effectiveness, durability, and comfort. From the selection of nylon or polyester to the use of high-performance fibers like Kevlar, every choice is grounded in scientific principles that ensure workers are protected in a variety of environments. By understanding the materials and processes behind harness construction, both safety professionals and workers can make better decisions about which harnesses best suit their specific needs.

Case Study: Shattered Glass, Shattered Trust – A Pharmaceutical Plant's Safety Crisis

A pharmaceutical plant was facing a crisis—a crisis that was more than just broken glass. It was about **broken trust and shattered confidence**.

The plant's workers were responsible for cleaning massive **glass vessels** used to manufacture life-saving medicines. They relied on safety harnesses to protect them during these tasks. But the very harnesses meant to keep them safe were part of the problem.

The Danger of Metal and Glass

The harnesses they used had **metal buckles, D-rings, and hooks**. In a confined space surrounded by delicate glass, one wrong move was all it took. A metal buckle would strike a vessel wall, and in an instant—**CRACK**. The glass would shatter.

Every break wasn't just a sound—it had far-reaching consequences:

➢ **Financial Losses:** More than 10 lacs spent on replacing the custom-made glass vessels.

➢ **Operational Delays:** Entire batches of medicine delayed or ruined, impacting patient care.

Reimagining the Harness

Our team at **I SSAFE** poured weeks of effort into innovation. We knew the answer lay in removing **every piece of metal** while maintaining safety and durability. We designed a new harness with:

➢ **High-Strength Textile Fittings:** Durable materials without any metal parts.

➢ **Soft, Flexible Webbing:** Non-abrasive webbing that wouldn't scratch or impact the glass surfaces.

We tested these harnesses under various conditions—mock cleanings, impact trials, and chemical exposure. The results spoke for themselves: the glass stayed intact, and the workers stayed safe.

Restoring Confidence

The plant adopted our new harnesses cautiously at first. But as the weeks turned into months, something remarkable happened:

➤ **No More Shattered Glass:** The glass vessels remained undamaged, free from accidental impacts.

➤ **Workers Relaxed:** The fear in the workers' eyes faded. They moved confidently, knowing their harnesses wouldn't betray them.

Operational Efficiency: No delays, no costly repairs, and no ruined batches of medicine. The plant operated smoothly and safely.

Chapter 6

Five Essential Considerations for Selecting the Right Harness

6.1 Introduction: The Importance of Selecting the Right Harness

Choosing the right safety harness is essential for ensuring worker protection, comfort, and compliance. A well-selected harness not only mitigates the risk of falls but also improves worker efficiency and satisfaction. This chapter delves into five fundamental considerations for selecting an appropriate harness: belt width, strength and durability, stitching quality, ergonomic design, and usability. Each of these factors plays a unique role in harness performance, contributing to the effectiveness of the equipment in various environments and industries. By understanding these elements, safety professionals and workers can make informed decisions, leading to better protection and improved work conditions.

6.2 Belt Width: The Foundation of Comfort and Safety

How Belt Width Affects Harness Performance

Belt width is a critical aspect of harness design, impacting both safety and comfort. A wider belt distributes force more evenly across the waist and back, reducing strain during prolonged use and providing additional lumbar support. Studies have shown that harnesses with belts between 2 to 4 inches in width offer the ideal balance between support and mobility, particularly for workers in construction and maintenance roles (American Society of Safety Professionals, 2020).

In the world of safety harness manufacturing, even the smallest adjustments in design can have monumental impacts on safety. Consider, for instance, the width of a harness's webbing—a detail that may seem inconsequential at first glance. Industry standards often recommend a width of 44mm for harness webbing, as this dimension is critical for distributing impact forces across the worker's body, reducing pressure points, and providing reliable support in a fall. Yet, some manufacturers quietly reduce this width by just 3-4mm in bulk production to save on material costs. Though the difference may be hard to detect, this subtle alteration can yield significant savings over time, potentially saving manufacturers thousands of dollars annually. With these savings, a manufacturer might afford luxuries—a new Mercedes, for instance—but at what cost to the worker?

For the worker trusting that harness with their life, that few-millimeter reduction could mean the difference between safety and tragedy. Narrower webbing compromises the structural integrity of the harness, reducing its ability to bear the load and absorb the force of a fall. The harness may fail under stress, resulting in life-threatening injuries or even death. And while no one may initially notice the width discrepancy, the consequences are painfully evident in an accident.

The reputational risks for companies engaging in such cost-cutting measures are immense. In 2019, a construction incident in New York highlighted the dangers of substandard harnesses. Investigations revealed that a thinner, weaker webbing had been used, contributing to a fatal fall. Such cases not only endanger lives but also expose companies to severe legal repercussions and reputational damage. Trust in a brand is built on the belief that safety is paramount, and cutting corners for profit betrays this trust.

For manufacturers committed to safety, it's essential to uphold rigorous standards. The small savings from reducing webbing width may seem enticing, but the long-term consequences of compromising worker safety—both in terms of human lives and business reputation—are too costly to bear. The importance of upholding safety standards and producing equipment that workers can rely on cannot be overstated.

Case Study: Fighting Back Pain – A Safety Harness That Supports Workers

Ramesh worked as a steelworker, often spending **10-12 hours a day** on construction sites, hanging from beams far high above the ground. Every morning, he put on his safety harness, ready for another tough shift. But by the middle of the afternoon, something familiar started to happen—his lower back began to ache. It wasn't just a little discomfort; it was a deep, constant pain that made it harder to focus and move.

The reason for the pain? His harness. The straps were stiff and didn't offer any real support for his back. Combined with the strain of holding tools and maintaining balance, his back pain grew unbearable. By the end of the day, Ramesh would stagger home, his back tight, his muscles sore, his morale low.

He wasn't the only one. Many of his colleagues faced the same problem. They relied on their safety harnesses to protect them from falls, but there was **nothing to protect their backs** from the daily strain. The pain wasn't just physical; it was a **mental and emotional drain**.

The Hidden Costs of Back Pain

The back pain caused by traditional safety harnesses wasn't just an inconvenience. It had serious consequences:

1. **Reduced Productivity** – As the pain set in, workers moved slower, which meant they completed fewer tasks and delayed work.

2. **Increased Sick Days** – Many workers had to take time off to rest and recover from their aching backs, slowing down projects and raising costs.

3. **Higher Injury Risk** – The constant pain made it harder for workers to maintain good posture and focus, which increased the chances of accidents on the job.

For companies, back pain among workers meant **lost time, increased costs, and declining morale**. For workers, it was a constant battle just to get through the day.

The I SSAFE Solution: Back Support Built In

Our team at I SSAFE worked hard to design a harness that would solve the back pain problem. Here's how we did it:

1. **Built-In Lumbar Support** – We added a **padded lumbar belt** designed to support the lower back, maintaining proper posture and reducing strain.

2. **Ergonomic Webbing Design** – The webbing was engineered to distribute weight evenly across the shoulders, back, and hips, reducing pressure on the lower spine.

3. **Adjustable Support Straps** – Workers could adjust the straps to ensure the harness fit snugly and comfortably, providing consistent back support throughout the day.

4. **Breathable Padding** – Soft, breathable padding reduced discomfort, preventing the harness from digging into the back during long shifts.

Once the new, back-support harnesses were introduced, the difference was clear. There were significant improvements in the workplace:

➢ **Fewer Sick Days** – Reduced back pain meant fewer workers taking time off.

➢ **Higher Morale** – Workers felt valued and cared for, boosting team spirit.

➢ **Increased Safety** – Less pain meant better focus, reducing workplace accidents.

For the first time, workers could perform their jobs without dreading the end-of-day backache. They went home not just safe, but **pain-free and proud** of their work.

Choosing the Right Belt Width for Specific Tasks

While wider belts provide better support, they may restrict movement in confined spaces or in jobs that require high agility. In these scenarios, a narrower belt is often preferable. For example, telecommunications workers may opt for a harness with a 2-inch belt to facilitate mobility when climbing towers, while workers engaged in heavy lifting may benefit from a 4-inch belt to reduce lumbar strain.

6.3   Stitching Quality: Securing Harness Integrity

Why Stitching is a Core Element of Safety

High-quality stitching is fundamental to a harness's structural integrity, as it holds the webbing and attachment points together under significant stress. ANSI guidelines mandate double or triple-stitching in critical areas, especially around D-rings and connection points, to enhance strength and durability. Bar-tack stitching, a method characterized by short, closely spaced stitches, is widely used in high-stress zones, such as around attachment points and load-bearing areas.

Inspection Tips for Stitching Quality

When selecting a harness, it is essential to inspect the stitching quality closely. Look for reinforced stitching in high-stress areas and contrasting thread colors, which make it easier to identify wear or fraying. Workers should check for loose threads or irregular stitching patterns, as these may indicate potential weak points.

In the manufacturing of safety harnesses, stitching isn't just a finishing touch—it's the lifeline holding the entire structure together. Each stitch reinforces the webbing, secures critical load-bearing points, and determines whether a harness will perform reliably under the immense force of a fall. Yet, some manufacturers cut corners by reducing the density or quality of stitching, aiming to save on both production time and costs. While a reduced stitch count might seem minor to those less familiar with harness construction, the impact on safety is profound.

Imagine a harness stitched with only a single line in critical areas, rather than the triple-stitched reinforcement specified by industry standards. In bulk production, reducing the stitching might shave a few seconds off the assembly time and save on thread costs, translating to significant savings over a production run. But at what risk? A harness with insufficient stitching can unravel or fail under strain, especially in high-stress areas like D-rings and connection points. In a fall, these weaker stitches might give way, leaving the worker unprotected at a very critical moment.

There are countless tragic examples of harnesses failing due to poor stitching. A construction incident in Texas in 2020 underscores the risk: a worker fell, and his harness—later found to have insufficient stitching in high-load areas—failed under the impact, leading to severe injuries. The company faced not only legal consequences but also a substantial loss in reputation, with clients and workers questioning their commitment to safety. For a brand, one incident like this can tarnish years of reputation and trust. And for the worker, it's a matter of life and health.

For manufacturers who truly care about safety, there's no room for cutting corners with stitching. We make sure to follow the highest stitching standards, often going beyond industry requirements, because we know that each and every thread plays a role in protecting lives. Skimping on stitching may yield small savings in the short term, but the long-term cost—potential harm to workers and damage to brand integrity—is far too high.

6.4 Ergonomic Design: Ensuring Comfort and Reducing Fatigue

Importance of Ergonomic Features in Harnesses

An ergonomic harness is designed to make wearing it more comfortable, which is especially important for workers who need to wear it for long hour. Features like padded shoulder straps, lumbar support, and adjustable components contribute to a comfortable fit, promoting compliance and enhancing worker productivity. Ergonomically designed harnesses help distribute weight evenly across the body, reducing pressure on the neck, shoulders, and lower back.

Research on How Ergonomics Improve Harness Design

A study conducted by the National Institute for Occupational Safety and Health (NIOSH) in 2020 found that ergonomically designed harnesses reduced self-reported discomfort and fatigue by 40% in construction workers, compared to standard harnesses without padding or lumbar support. Workers who wore the more comfortable, ergonomic harnesses were much more likely to wear them properly and consistently. This comfort led to better safety and fewer accidents.

Case Study: The Hidden Struggle of Safety Harnesses – From Pain to Protection

Ravi was a construction worker, spending 10 hours a day high up on scaffolding, hundreds of feet above the ground. Every morning, he strapped on his safety harness—a routine that was supposed to bring him security. But for Ravi, and thousands like him, the harness was a source of discomfort, fatigue, and silent frustration.

By lunchtime, the harness's **straps dug into his shoulders**, leaving red marks that hurt whenever he moved. The **thigh straps** squeezed so tightly that his legs went numb. The weight of the harness pressed on his **back and abdomen**, making it hard to breathe freely. And during longer shifts, the discomfort became unbearable.

But Ravi couldn't complain. Safety was non-negotiable, and like everyone else, he just pushed through the pain.

The Problems Ravi Faced:

1. **Fatigue and Pain** – Constant pressure and discomfort drained his energy, slowing his work.

2. **Loss of Focus** – The pain made it hard for him to concentrate, increasing the chances of mistakes.

3. **Long-Term Damage** – The continuous pressure caused muscle strain, joint pain, and circulation issues.

Ravi's safety harness was supposed to protect him, but it was actually harming his health in ways that no one seemed to talked about.

Our solution was built around three key innovations:

1. **Ergonomic Design** – The harness was engineered to distribute weight evenly across the body, reducing pressure points on the **shoulders, thighs, and abdomen**.

2. **Padded Straps** – We added soft, durable padding to the straps to prevent them from rubbing and causing discomfort during long hours of wear.

3. **Breathable Materials** – The webbing was made from lightweight, breathable fabric to keep workers cool and reduce sweat buildup.

Every detail was tested and refined. The goal was simple: a harness that workers could wear all day without pain.

The Outcome: Comfort and Safety Combined

When Ravi first put on the new harness, he expected the same discomfort. But as the hours passed, he felt a difference:

➢ **No More Pressure Points** – The padding cushioned his shoulders and thighs.

➢ **Better Mobility** – He could move freely without the straps digging into his body.

➢ **Less Fatigue** – By the end of the day, he wasn't drained or in pain.

His work improved. He focused better, worked faster, and felt safer. For the first time, his harness wasn't just a lifeline; it was a tool that respected his body.

6.5 Usability and Functionality: Key Features for Operational Efficiency

Quick-Connect Buckles and Adjustment Points

For workers who frequently put on and remove their harnesses, usability features like quick-connect buckles and multiple adjustment points enhance convenience and safety. Quick-connect buckles operate similarly to seatbelts, allowing for secure attachment without needing to thread the straps through buckles manually. Adjustable points on the shoulders, chest, and legs enable a customized fit, essential for preventing slippage or discomfort.

Additional Features for Specific Job Requirements

Some harnesses are designed with specialized features tailored to certain job functions. For instance:

➢ **Tool Loops and Attachment Points:** Common in harnesses for utility and construction workers who carry tools while working at heights.

➢ **Reflective Strips:** Important for nighttime or low-visibility environments, ensuring that workers remain visible to others.

➢ **Integrated Lanyard Keepers:** Convenient storage for lanyards when they're not in use, reducing tripping hazards.

6.6 Conclusion: The Essentials of a Reliable Safety Harness

Selecting the right harness is not just a matter of meeting compliance; it's a strategic choice that impacts safety, comfort, and efficiency. By considering belt width, material durability, stitching quality, ergonomic design, and usability features, employers and workers can ensure that they choose harnesses that align with their specific needs and environmental conditions. These five considerations form the foundation of a safe, efficient, and productive work environment, where workers are empowered to perform their tasks confidently and securely.

○　○　○　○

Chapter 7

Innovations and Problem Solving

7.1 Introduction: The Need for Continuous Innovation in Safety Harness Design

The safety harness industry is continually evolving to meet the demands of modern work environments and address recurring issues such as sizing, comfort, and functionality. As industries grow more complex and diverse, harness manufacturers are developing new technologies and materials to create products that are not only safer but also more user-friendly. This chapter examines recent innovations in safety harness design, focusing on how these advancements solve common problems and improve the safety, comfort, and usability of harnesses for workers in high-risk settings.

7.2 Addressing Sizing Issues: One Size Doesn't Fit All

Challenges of Sizing in Safety Harnesses

Historically, many safety harnesses were designed with a "one-size-fits-all" approach, which often failed to accommodate the diverse body types found in today's workforce. Poorly fitted harnesses can lead to discomfort, reduced mobility, and even safety risks, as they may not secure the wearer effectively. According to a 2021 report by the Occupational Safety and Health Administration (OSHA), ill-fitting harnesses contribute to 10% of all fall-related injuries due to improper force distribution and strap positioning (OSHA, 2021).

Innovations in Adjustable and Inclusive Sizing

To combat these issues, manufacturers have introduced adjustable harnesses that offer a wider range of sizes, from small to extra-large, and include more customizable fitting options. Some modern harnesses feature extended adjustability points on the shoulders, chest, and legs, allowing for a better, more personalized fit. Additionally, some companies are developing harnesses specifically designed for women, addressing anatomical differences to provide better comfort and security. These innovations aim to make harnesses more inclusive and practical for diverse users.

Case Study: Redefining Safety for Women – Comfort, Fit, and Freedom

Meena, one of the few women working at a major construction site, spent her days scaling scaffolding and managing critical tasks at height. Every morning, she strapped on her safety harness, but it wasn't made for her. Instead of support, the harness brought discomfort and frustration.

The harness, designed for men, pressed uncomfortably against her **chest and bust**, making movement difficult and awkward. The rigid webbing cut into her **shoulders**, adding to the strain of carrying tools and equipment. Long shifts became a nightmare as the harness dug into her **groin and thighs**, causing discomfort that grew unbearable.

She pushed through the pain, determined to prove herself in a male-dominated field. But the discomfort was relentless, and it wasn't just physical—it was **demoralizing**. She felt trapped in a design that didn't consider her body, her needs, or her dignity.

The Hidden Flaws of One-Size-Fits-All Designs

Traditional harnesses were built with a **one-size-fits-all** mindset, but they failed to account for women's unique anatomy. Meena's struggles highlighted the major issues:

1. **Chest Discomfort** – Straps pressed tightly against her bust, causing pain and restricted movement.

2. **Shoulder Strain** – Rigid webbing placed excessive weight on her shoulders, leading to fatigue.

3. **Groin Pressure** – Tight thigh straps created painful pressure in the **groin area**, making long hours unbearable.

The I SSAFE Solution: Tailored for Women

After extensive research, testing over 14 different comfort models, and collecting feedback, we developed a harness with these key innovations:

1. **Elasticated Webbing Near the Bust** – The webbing was designed with **flexible, elasticated material** to accommodate different bust sizes, providing support without tightness or discomfort.

2. **Elasticated Shoulder Straps** – These straps reduced pressure and allowed for a **more even weight distribution**, preventing shoulder fatigue.

3. **Padded Groin Straps** – Soft, ergonomic padding in the thigh and groin areas eliminated discomfort, making long shifts manageable.

This harness is designed to prioritize safety and comfort, specifically addressing the unique needs of women in the workplace.

7.3 Enhancing Comfort: Ergonomic and Breathable Materials

The Importance of Comfort in Safety Compliance

Uncomfortable harnesses often result in workers being hesitant to wear them correctly or consistently, leading to reduced safety compliance. Traditional harnesses often use materials that, while strong, lack breathability, causing heat buildup and discomfort. This is particularly problematic for outdoor workers exposed to high temperatures or those engaged in physically demanding tasks.

Advancements in Breathable, Moisture-Wicking Materials

To address these challenges, manufacturers are now using breathable, moisture-wicking materials into harness designs. Materials such as mesh and specially engineered synthetic fibers enhance airflow, allowing the harness to remain comfortable even in warm conditions. A 2020 study by the Ergonomics Society found that harnesses made from breathable materials reduced heat stress symptoms by 30% among workers in construction, compared to traditional harnesses.

Integrating Padding for Pressure Relief

Another advancement in comfort-focused design is the addition of strategically placed padding around the shoulders, thighs, and back. This padding is made from lightweight, impact-absorbing materials, which help reduce pressure points and minimize fatigue during extended use.

7.4 Solving Common Discomfort Issues: Reducing Pressure Points and Chafing

Ergonomically Designed Straps

Safety harnesses are now available with ergonomically contoured straps that reduce pressure on sensitive areas like the shoulders and thighs. These contoured designs allow the harness to move more naturally with the body, which prevents chafing and minimizes restriction of movement. Manufacturers are also experimenting with soft, skin-friendly materials for harness straps, significantly reducing friction against the skin.

7.5 Innovations in Lightweight Design: Reducing Harness Weight

Reducing Harness Weight for Enhanced Mobility

For jobs that require frequent movement or climbing, such as telecommunications or utility work, heavy harnesses can feel restrictive. To address this, manufacturers are now designing lightweight harnesses using advanced polymers and high-strength fibers that maintain durability while reducing overall weight. These lightweight materials are especially beneficial for industries that demand agility, as they reduce worker fatigue and improve mobility.

7.6 Conclusion: The Future of Safety Harness Innovation

Innovations in safety harness design are transforming these devices from basic protective equipment into multi-functional tools that enhance both safety and efficiency. From smart harnesses with real-time monitoring to lightweight designs that reduce fatigue, these advancements address the challenges faced by modern workers in diverse environments. As technology continues to evolve, safety harnesses will likely become even more integrated with digital systems, offering new levels of protection and operational insight. By understanding and embracing these innovations, industries can equip their workforce with harnesses that not only meet but exceed safety standards, ensuring a safer and more productive workplace.

O O O O

Chapter 8

Maintenance and Care

8.1 Introduction: The Role of Maintenance in Safety Harness Longevity

Safety harnesses are complex devices designed to protect lives, but their effectiveness depends on their condition. Proper maintenance and regular inspections are crucial to ensuring that harnesses perform reliably in high-risk situations. This chapter provides a comprehensive guide to maintaining and caring for safety harnesses, emphasizing the importance of regular inspections, proper cleaning, and timely replacement. By understanding and implementing these practices, companies can enhance the lifespan of their harnesses and, most importantly, protect their workforce.

8.2 Daily Inspections: The First Line of Defense

Importance of Daily Pre-Use Checks

Before each use, workers should inspect their harnesses to identify any signs of wear, damage, or compromised functionality. Daily inspections act as the first line of defense, helping catch minor issues before they escalate into serious safety risks. According to OSHA guidelines, workers must conduct a visual inspection of all harness components, including webbing, buckles, D-rings, and stitching, to confirm that the equipment is in safe working condition (OSHA, 2021).

Inspection Checklist for Workers

Daily inspections should include:

- **Webbing:** Check for fraying, cuts, burns, or areas of discoloration that could indicate weakened fibers.

- **D-Rings and Buckles:** Ensure that these components are free of rust, deformation, or cracks.

- **Stitching:** Look for loose or broken stitches, particularly around load-bearing areas.

- **Labels and Tags:** Verify that identification labels are legible, as these provide crucial information for traceability and compliance.

8.3 Cleaning and Storage: Extending Harness Lifespan

Proper Cleaning Techniques

Regular cleaning is essential for maintaining harnesses in good condition, as dirt, chemicals, and moisture can degrade materials over time. To ensure your harness remains safe and durable, it is recommended to clean it by hand with mild soap and water. Harsh detergents, bleach, and machine washing should be avoided, as they can weaken the webbing and compromise the harness's structural integrity.

Step-by-Step Cleaning Process

1. **Soak:** Submerge the harness in a solution of mild soap and lukewarm water, allowing dirt to loosen.

2. **Scrub Gently:** Use a soft brush to clean the webbing, ensuring you don't scrub too hard, as this could damage the fibers.

3. **Rinse Thoroughly:** Rinse the harness completely to remove all soap residue, as residual chemicals can degrade the material.

4. **Dry Properly:** Hang the harness in a well-ventilated area, away from direct sunlight or high heat, to allow it to dry naturally and completely.

8.4 Storage Best Practices: Preventing Premature Wear

Ideal Storage Conditions for Safety Harnesses

Correct storage is crucial to prevent harness deterioration. Harnesses should be stored in cool, dry locations, away from direct sunlight, chemicals, and sharp objects that could damage the materials. A designated storage area, such as a locker or hanging rack, keeps harnesses organized and minimizes exposure to environmental hazards.

Protecting Harnesses from Environmental Hazards

Exposure to UV light, extreme temperatures, and chemicals can weaken the harness over time. Ultraviolet radiation is especially harmful, causing materials like nylon and polyester to degrade and lose tensile strength. By storing harnesses in areas free from direct sunlight and away from chemical storage, you protect them from damage and maintain their durability, ensuring they remain safe and effective when needed.

Extra Tip: Regularly check your storage area for any risks like moisture or extreme temperature changes, which could also affect your harness's integrity. Taking these precautions now can save you from costly replacements later.

8.5   Recognizing When to Replace a Harness: Indicators of Wear and Tear

Signs That a Harness Needs Replacement

Even with proper care, all harnesses have a finite lifespan. Recognizing when it's time to replace a harness is crucial for maintaining worker safety. Look for these signs:

➢ **Fraying or Broken Fibers:** Any visible damage to the webbing, such as frayed edges, cuts, or holes, indicates wear that can weaken the harness.

➢ **Rust or Corrosion on Metal Parts:** Rusted or corroded D-rings, buckles, or adjusters can compromise structural integrity.

➢ **Compromised Stitching:** Loose, broken, or missing stitches, particularly around areas that bear heavy loads, can lead to failure during use.

➢ **Fading Labels and Illegible Tags:** If the manufacturer's labels are worn or illegible, the harness may not meet regulatory compliance requirements.

Case Study: Breaking the Cycle of Corrosion and Waste

On a hot July afternoon, we received a message at **I SSAFE** about a fertilizer plant's safety harnesses deteriorating every **10-11 months** due to extreme chemical exposure.

Each harness was a casualty of **corrosion**—metal buckles chipping, webbing weakening, trust breaking. Every replacement cycle drained the team's **time, energy, and morale**. Workers had to be retrained, procurement processes restarted, and old harnesses discarded, adding to environmental waste.

The frustration was palpable. Safety wasn't the issue—they were following protocols—but the constant breakdown left workers doubting their gear. And when you're working in hazardous conditions, doubt is dangerous.

A Cycle of Frustration and Waste

In the fertilizer plant, workers were surrounded by a toxic mix of **sulfuric acid, ammonia, and phosphoric acid**. These chemicals didn't just wear down the equipment—they wore down **confidence and productivity**. The harnesses barely lasted 11 months before the webbing frayed and the metal components corroded.

Each replacement cycle was exhaustive: inspections, paperwork, new fittings, and training. The discarded harnesses piled up—a painful reminder of the waste they couldn't avoid. The **environment paid the price**, and so did the workers' morale.

A Promise to Find a Solution

Our team at I SSAFE got to work. We examined the corroded harnesses, studied the plant's environment, and brainstormed relentlessly. We needed a harness that could withstand the harshest chemicals without compromising safety or adding to the waste problem.

Engineering Trust

We developed a solution that changed everything:

We tested these harnesses under extreme conditions: acid baths, chemical mists, and tensile stress. They held up where others had failed.

When we shipped the harnesses to the fertilizer plant, we held our breath, hoping they would withstand the challenge.

Breaking Free

Months later, we received an update. The new harnesses had lasted through **10 months, 11, 12—and beyond**. No fraying. No chipping. No endless replacements. The harnesses endured for **22 months**—double the lifespan.

The plant finally broke free from the cycle of frustration. The discarded harnesses no longer piled up, easing the burden on the environment.

One simple message followed:

"You didn't just give us harnesses. You gave us back our trust, our time, and our hope."

8.6 Conclusion: Ensuring Safety Through Rigorous Maintenance

Proper maintenance and care of safety harnesses are non-negotiable elements of workplace safety. Through daily inspections, scheduled professional checks, appropriate cleaning, and careful storage, companies can ensure that harnesses remain safe and effective for their intended lifespan. Training workers to recognize wear and understand the importance of timely replacement further strengthens this safety approach, creating a work environment where every employee can trust their equipment.

Ultimately, a proactive approach to harness maintenance not only extends the life of the equipment but also significantly enhances worker safety. This, in turn, fosters a culture of responsibility and protection, ensuring a safer and more efficient workplace for all.

Chapter 9

Compliance and Legal Standards

9.1 Introduction: The Essential Role of Compliance in Harness Safety

Compliance with regulatory standards is a foundational element of the safety harness industry. Meeting these standards ensures that harnesses are designed, manufactured, and used in ways that protect workers and minimize risks. For companies, adherence to legal requirements is not only a matter of regulatory necessity but also of ethical responsibility. This chapter outlines the primary compliance and legal standards governing safety harnesses, examining the role of organizations such as OSHA and ANSI. It also explores the potential consequences of non-compliance, emphasizing the importance of adherence to keep workers safe and maintain organizational integrity.

9.2 Understanding Key Regulatory Bodies and Standards

OSHA (Occupational Safety and Health Administration)

In the United States, OSHA is the leading regulatory body responsible for workplace safety standards, including fall protection requirements. OSHA mandates that all employers provide appropriate fall protection systems, which include harnesses, for employees working at heights of six feet or more in the construction industry and four feet in general industry (OSHA, 2021). Additionally, OSHA also enforces strict guidelines on equipment inspections, use, and training, aiming to minimize the risk of falls, which remain the leading cause of death in construction. By ensuring compliance, OSHA helps protect workers and supports a safer working environment.

ANSI (American National Standards Institute)

ANSI develops voluntary standards that enhance workplace safety and often go beyond OSHA's minimum requirements. ANSI's Z359 series of standards address various aspects of fall protection and personal protective equipment (PPE). The ANSI Z359.1 standard, for example, specifies requirements for safety harness design, testing, and performance, mandating a minimum tensile strength of 5,000 pounds for webbing and D-rings to ensure reliable load-bearing capacity. ANSI standards are frequently adopted by many companies seeking to maintain high safety standards, even when OSHA compliance alone may suffice. By following these standards, businesses can go beyond the basics, ensuring better protection for their workers.

CE- EN Standards (European Norms)

In Europe, harness manufacturers and users follow the EN standards, particularly EN 361, which sets requirements for full-body harnesses. These standards also specify testing methods and minimum safety requirements, similar to those of ANSI and OSHA. The European market's rigorous

EN compliance highlights the increasing globalization of safety standards, as many companies aim to meet both EN and ANSI standards to appeal to a broader market. This global standardization ensures consistent safety levels and strengthens protection for workers worldwide.

BIS (Bureau of Indian Standards Norms) - ISI Mark for India

The **Bureau of Indian Standards (BIS)**, known for its ISI mark (Indian Standards Institution), is India's national standards organization responsible for establishing and maintaining standards for safety, quality, and reliability across various industries, including PPE. In India, harnesses intended for fall protection must meet BIS standards, which align with global best practices while also considering local working conditions. The BIS certification, denoted by the ISI mark, signifies that the harness has undergone extensive testing to meet safety, durability, and performance standards. This certification process includes assessments of material strength, stitching quality, and the functionality of components like D-rings and buckles.

BIS compliance is critical for manufacturers in the Indian market, as it assures customers and regulatory bodies that the products adhere to India's specific safety requirements. The ISI mark is widely recognized as a symbol of quality and safety, and BIS-certified harnesses are mandatory for certain sectors, such as construction, oil and gas, and industrial manufacturing.

9.3 Compliance Requirements for Safety Harness Manufacturing

Materials and Construction Standards

Compliance standards specify the materials and construction techniques required to make harnesses safe and durable. For example, ANSI mandates that safety harnesses use high-strength materials like nylon and polyester for webbing and durable metals for D-rings and buckles. The EN standards add that harnesses should be tested under extreme conditions, such as exposure to chemicals and UV radiation, to ensure durability in various environments. Manufacturers who prioritize compliance often conduct rigorous in-house testing to confirm that their products meet or exceed these standards, thus building trust with both regulatory bodies and end-users.

Testing and Quality Assurance

To achieve certification, harnesses must pass various tests simulating real-life conditions, including tensile strength, drop tests, and corrosion resistance. ANSI Z359.7 outlines the methods for testing safety equipment, requiring harnesses to withstand force levels significantly higher than typical fall impacts. Quality assurance processes ensure that each harness meets these requirements, reducing the risk of failure during use. Manufacturers who adhere to ANSI and EN standards regularly test their products to maintain certification and ensure ongoing compliance with the latest regulations.

This commitment to testing and quality assurance not only strengthens safety but also instills confidence in users, knowing that the harnesses they rely on have been built to the highest standards.

9.4 Legal Implications of Non-Compliance

Consequences for Manufacturers

Failure to meet compliance standards can result in severe legal consequences for manufacturers. Non-compliant products may be subject to recalls, fines, and potential lawsuits, especially if they lead to accidents or fatalities. In 2020, a safety equipment manufacturer faced a $1 million lawsuit after a harness failure resulted in injury; the investigation revealed that the harness did not meet ANSI Z359 requirements. This incident highlighted the critical importance of maintaining compliance, as non-compliant products not only jeopardize lives but also expose companies to significant financial and reputational damage.

Employer Liability and Legal Obligations

Employers who fail to provide compliant fall protection equipment can face penalties under OSHA regulations. In the case of a fall-related injury or death, companies may be subject to fines, increased insurance costs, and lawsuits filed by injured workers or their families. In 2019, OSHA fined a roofing contractor over $500,000 after an investigation revealed that they had provided substandard harnesses, contributing to a fatal accident. Legal consequences like these underscores the importance of investing in compliant equipment and maintaining rigorous safety protocols.

9.5 Conclusion: The Critical Importance of Compliance in Harness Safety

In conclusion, compliance with safety harness standards is crucial for protecting workers and maintaining a safe work environment. Adhering to regulations set by organizations like OSHA, ANSI, EN, and BIS ensures harnesses are durable, reliable, and effective. Non-compliance can lead to serious legal and financial consequences, making it essential for manufacturers and employers to prioritize safety and meet regulatory standards to safeguard lives and build trust.

Chapter 10

The Future of Safety Harness Technology

10.1 Introduction: The Evolution of Safety Harness Innovation

The safety harness industry is on the brink of transformative advancements. With emerging technologies and evolving user demands, harnesses are shifting from simple protective devices to smart, multifunctional systems that address a wider range of safety and ergonomic needs. This chapter explores the future of safety harness technology, focusing on innovations in materials, digital integration, and user-centered design. As we look ahead, it's clear that the harnesses of tomorrow will not only improve safety but also enhance efficiency, worker comfort, and overall job satisfaction.

10.2 Integration of Smart Technology: The Rise of Connected Harnesses

Real-Time Monitoring with Embedded Sensors

The future of safety harnesses is increasingly driven by smart technology, with embedded sensors capable of tracking real-time data. These sensors monitor critical parameters, such as a worker's position, movement, and even environmental conditions. In the event of a fall, smart harnesses can automatically send alerts to the safety team, allowing for faster response times and potentially preventing serious injuries.

Smart Harness Applications in High-Risk Environments

In high-risk environments like oil rigs or telecommunications towers, the use of GPS-enabled smart harnesses can greatly improve safety monitoring. By providing real-time location data, these harnesses help ensure workers are always within safe zones and alert safety teams to any dangerous deviations. This integration of smart technology not only boosts safety but also improves efficiency by providing crucial data for ongoing risk assessments and decision-making.

10.3 Harnesses with Health Monitoring Capabilities

Tracking Worker Health Metrics

Future harnesses will likely incorporate sensors to track health metrics such as heart rate, hydration levels, and fatigue indicators. This technology will be particularly beneficial in physically demanding industries, where risks like overexertion and dehydration are common. Health-monitoring harnesses could alert workers and supervisors if vital signs indicate danger, potentially preventing accidents due to physical exhaustion or heat stress.

10.4 Personalized and Custom-Fit Harnesses Using 3D Scanning

The Rise of Custom-Fit Safety Harnesses

As body diversity becomes a greater consideration, manufacturers are exploring 3D scanning technology to create custom-fit harnesses tailored to each worker's unique body shape. Custom-fit harnesses offer improved comfort, reduced pressure points, and enhanced safety, as a perfectly fitted harness is less likely to slip or shift during use. This personalized approach ensures that every worker has the best possible protection and comfort, helping reduce the risk of accidents caused by poorly fitted gear.

Pilot Program: Custom-Fit Harnesses in Aviation

A 2021 pilot program in the aviation maintenance industry used 3D scanning to create custom-fit harnesses for workers of varying sizes. The custom-fit harnesses reduced discomfort and improved mobility, leading to a 30% increase in worker satisfaction. This success story demonstrates the potential for custom-fit harnesses to enhance comfort, compliance, and overall safety across industries. As the technology evolves, we can expect more industries to adopt these tailored solutions, ensuring that safety harnesses become even more effective and inclusive.

10.5 Environmentally Adaptive Harnesses: Responding to Extreme Conditions

Harnesses Designed for Specific Environmental Challenges

Future harnesses may be designed to adapt to extreme conditions, such as sub-zero temperatures or high humidity.

Through materials engineering, companies are developing harnesses that remain flexible in freezing temperatures, as well as those that resist moisture and chemical exposure. For example, harnesses made with thermally adaptive materials can retain elasticity and durability, even in harsh climates.

10.6 Conclusion: A Future of Smarter, Safer, and More Sustainable Harnesses

The future of safety harness technology promises is set to revolutionize the industry with harnesses that are lighter, stronger, and more adaptive to individual needs and environmental challenges. As materials science advances, digital technology becomes more integrated, and customized fits become possible, safety harnesses will not only continue to protect workers but also enhance their comfort and well-being. For manufacturers, embracing these innovations is both a responsibility and an opportunity to lead the industry toward a new era of safety.

Harnesses that anticipate and address worker needs will redefine what it means to prioritize safety, ensuring that every ascent is secure, every job is comfortable, and every worker returns home safely. As the industry evolves, the focus will shift from simply protecting workers to providing a comprehensive solution that prioritizes both safety and well-being, paving the way for a future where harnesses play a pivotal role in creating safer, more efficient workplaces.

Case Study: Reducing the Burden – Lightweight Comfort in Oil and Gas Safety Harnesses

The Weight They Carried

Deep in the oil fields of the Gulf, every shift started with a ritual: strapping into a safety harness. For workers like Arjun, this routine was both essential and exhausting. The harness, designed to protect him while working at heights and over precarious platforms, was an **unseen burden** he carried every day.

Weighing over **3.5 kilograms**, with thick, rigid webbing and bulky metal fittings, the harness seemed to grow heavier as the hours passed. Combined with the tools and equipment strapped to his waist, Arjun often felt like he was carrying the weight of the job on his back—literally.

By midday, his **shoulders ached**, his **thighs felt pinched**, and his **lower back throbbed** from the strain. The harness restricted his movements, slowed his pace, and drained his energy.

The I SSAFE Solution: Lightening the Load

We set to work designing a harness specifically for the demands of the oil and gas industry. The goal was to reduce weight without compromising safety. After rigorous research and testing, we delivered a solution that addressed every pain point:

1. **Lightweight Webbing** – We used **high-strength, low-weight polyester webbing,** which reduced the overall harness weight by **30%**.

2. **Ergonomic Design** – The harness was engineered to distribute weight evenly across the body, reducing strain on the **shoulders, back, and thighs**.

3. **Composite Fittings** – Instead of traditional metal buckles, we used **high-strength polymer fittings**, cutting down the weight while maintaining durability and safety standards.

4. **Padded Straps** – Soft, breathable padding was added to key pressure points, preventing chafing and reducing discomfort during long shifts.

The Results: Freedom to Work

The new harness was a revelation. Arjun noticed the difference immediately. The harness was **light flexible, and comfortable**—almost as if it wasn't there. By the end of his shift, he remained alert, his muscles weren't screaming, and his back wasn't aching.

Across the site, workers reported:

➢ **Less Fatigue** – Energy levels remained high throughout their shifts.

➢ **Increased Mobility** – Moving, climbing, and bending became effortless.

➢ **Improved Safety** – Fewer mistakes and near-misses, thanks to better focus and comfort.

By addressing comfort and reducing fatigue, the new design not only boosted performance but also made a significant impact on worker safety, demonstrating that innovation in harness design can enhance both productivity and well-being.

Conclusion:
A Commitment to Safety at Every Level

As we close this comprehensive guide on safety harnesses, it's evident that harnesses are far more than mere compliance tools—they are life-saving devices central to modern workplace safety. By understanding the intricate components, careful design, and rigorous standards that define a high-quality safety harness, manufacturers, employers, and workers alike are better equipped to make informed decisions that prioritize safety, comfort, and reliability. Ultimately, investing in the right harness ensures not only compliance but the protection and well-being of every worker on the job.

A Journey from Basic Compliance to Complete Safety

Throughout this book, we've explored the development of safety harnesses from simple belts designed for fall protection to advanced, ergonomic systems that integrate cutting-edge materials and smart technology. Today's harnesses are the result of decades of innovation and a strong commitment to worker well-being, highlighting the fact that safety is a shared responsibility at every level—from manufacturing and engineering to daily use and maintenance.

Reinforcing Safety Through Quality and Integrity

The integrity of a safety harness depends on the quality of its materials, stitching, and design. When manufacturers uphold stringent quality standards, they create products that workers can trust in critical moments. On the other hand, when corners are cut—whether in webbing width, stitching, or inspection—the safety of the worker is compromised, with potentially tragic consequences. As we've discussed, maintaining compliance with regulatory bodies like OSHA and ANSI, and even going beyond these standards, reinforces trust, ensures durability, and safeguards lives. These efforts are far more valuable than any short-term savings gained by sacrificing quality.

Embracing Innovation and Continuous Improvement

The future of safety harnesses lies in continual innovation. Advancements in smart technology, eco-friendly materials, and ergonomic designs open new pathways for enhancing worker protection. With harnesses now equipped with sensors, GPS, and health monitoring features, the industry is moving toward a new era of proactive safety management. Manufacturers committed to innovation and excellence will lead this transformation, helping redefine industry standards and supporting workers more effectively.

Building a Safety-First Culture

The effective use of safety harnesses also depends on a robust culture of safety within organizations. Employers who invest in training, foster open communication about safety concerns, and empower workers to take responsibility for their well-being set the stage for safer, more productive workplaces. A safety-first culture, as discussed, is a foundation upon which all other safety practices are built. By encouraging leaders to model safety behavior and implementing policies like the Stop-Work Authority, organizations send a clear message that every employee has the right to a safe work environment.

Looking Ahead: A Vision for the Future

As industries continue to evolve, the role of safety harnesses will only grow in importance. With an increasing focus on sustainability, technology, and personalized design, harnesses will become even more adaptive to workers' needs and environmental conditions. Companies that embrace these changes and make safety an integral part of their identity will thrive, benefiting from a loyal workforce and a strong reputation. Safety is not just a regulatory requirement—it is a fundamental right of every worker, and the responsibility to uphold it rests with everyone involved.

Final Thoughts

"Mastering Safety Harnesses: From Compliance to Comfort, A Comprehensive Guide" is more than a manual—it's a call to action for manufacturers, employers, and workers to take safety seriously. By investing in high-quality equipment, adhering to rigorous standards, and fostering a culture of continuous improvement, we create workplaces where every worker can focus on their tasks with confidence, knowing their safety is a priority. As we move forward, let

us remember that even the smallest detail—whether it's a stitch or a material choice—can make the biggest difference. Together, through dedication to safety and innovation, we can ensure that every ascent is secure, every task is completed confidently, and every worker returns home safely.

This conclusion serves as a strong, inspiring finish to the guide, summarizing key insights and reinforcing the essential nature of safety in the harness industry. It highlights the shared responsibility in workplace safety and the ongoing commitment required from all parties to make this vision a reality.

Strengthen Your Safety Harness (Literally)!

In my years of experience in the weaving industry, I've developed a deep passion for creating products that offer both quality and safety. Now, as I step into the safety harness industry, I bring that expertise with me. I know exactly how to make safety harnesses 200% stronger, ensuring maximum durability and protection.

Because you're a reader of this book, I want to offer you something special. My mission is to help businesses design and improve their safety harnesses to make them safer and more reliable.

Let's connect for a 1-2-1 discussion where I'll share my insights on how you can enhance your harness designs.

Email: ashishmittal@issafe.in

Let's strengthen your harnesses together!

Best Regards,

Ashish K Mittal

Appendices

Appendix A: Glossary of Key Terms

This glossary provides definitions of important terms used throughout the book, assisting readers in navigating industry-specific language and technical concepts related to safety harnesses and fall protection systems.

ANSI (American National Standards Institute)
A private, non-profit organization that oversees the development of voluntary safety and health standards in the United States, including those for personal protective equipment such as safety harnesses. The ANSI Z359 standards are essential for fall protection compliance.

1. **Breaking Strength:** The maximum force that a material, such as harness webbing, can withstand before failing. Safety harness components like webbing and D-rings are tested to withstand specific breaking strengths, typically around 5,000 pounds, to ensure they hold up during a fall.

2. **D-Ring:** A metal ring typically located on the back, chest, or hips of a harness, used as an attachment point for fall arrest lanyards, lifelines, or positioning devices.

3. **Fall Arrest:** A system designed to stop a fall safely. It includes a harness, connectors, and anchor points, preventing the wearer from reaching the ground and reducing impact forces on the body.

4. **Harness Webbing:** A strong, woven material that forms the main body of a safety harness, providing support and absorbing impact forces. Common materials include nylon, polyester, and high-strength fibers like Kevlar.

5. **OSHA (Occupational Safety and Health Administration):** A U.S. government agency responsible for setting and enforcing workplace safety regulations. OSHA mandates fall protection requirements for employers in industries where workers face height-related risks.

6. **Shock Absorber:** A device or element within a fall arrest system that limits impact forces during a fall. Shock-absorbing lanyards, for example, contain materials that stretch to reduce the impact force on the body.

7. **Stop-Work Authority:** A policy allowing workers to stop work if they observe unsafe conditions or potential hazards, promoting a proactive approach to safety.

○　○　○　○